Name Above All Names

AN INVITATION TO REMEMBER WHO JESUS REALLY IS

JAZMIN N. FRANK

© 2019 Jazmin N. Frank

Printed in the United States of America

All rights reserved. No portion of this book may be reproduced, stored in a retrieval system, or transmitted in any form or by any means—electronic, mechanical, photocopy, recording, scanning, or other—without the prior written permission of the publisher. The only exception is brief quotations in printed reviews and certain other noncommercial uses permitted by copyright law.

www.jazminnfrank.com

Cover & interior design by Typewriter Creative Co. Hanging lights illustration by Jasmine Smith.

Scripture quotations are from the ESV® Bible (The Holy Bible, English Standard Version®), copyright © 2001 by Crossway, a publishing ministry of Good News Publishers. Used by permission. All rights reserved.

ISBN 978-0-578-57998-6 (Paperback)

To Frederick. Thank you for being a spiritual father to me and for your example of faithfulness and love. You are a blessing to so many.

To Stephanie, Jacob, Carolyn, Michael, Amanda, Ruthie, Mary Carlyn, Charles, and Elena. Thank you for making space for me, for calling out my gifts, and encouraging me in this calling to write. Your support, prayers, encouragement, and couches mean the world to me.

STUDYING WITH A GROUP?
DOWNLOAD THE FREE LEADER GUIDE AT
HTTPS://JAZMINNFRANK.COM/GROUP

Table of Contents

Introduction — 7

Bible Study Basics — 9

DAY 1: Jesus Christ — 13

DAY 2: Word — 17

DAY 3: True Light — 21

DAY 4: Lamb of God — 27

DAY 5: Rabbi — 31

DAY 6: Son of God — 37

DAY 7: Sovereign — 43

DAY 8: Temple — 47

DAY 9: Son of Man — 51

DAY 10: Savior of the World — 57

DAY 11: Healer — 61

DAY 12: Son — 65

DAY 13: Bread — 71

DAY 14: Christ — 77

DAY 15:	I AM	81
DAY 16:	Light of the World	85
DAY 17:	Good Shepherd	89
DAY 18:	Resurrection and the Life	93
DAY 19:	Annointed King	97
DAY 20:	Light	101
DAY 21:	Servant	105
DAY 22:	Way. Truth, Life	111
DAY 23:	True Vine	115
DAY 24:	Overcomer	119
DAY 25:	High Priest	123
DAY 26:	King of the Jews	129
DAY 27:	Fulfillment	133
DAY 28:	Lord	139
DAY 29:	My Lord... My God	143
DAY 30:	Redeemer and Restorer	149
DAY 31:	My Jesus	153
	A Note from the Author	159
	Notes & Resources	161

Introduction

Sometimes I forget who Jesus is.

I forget in seasons when life is tossing me here and there and all I want to do is grab hold of something solid.

I forget him in seasons when I feel like I got this and I am confident and independent and totally capable of doing life on my own.

I forget him in seasons when nothing especially spectacular is happening and everything just feels very routine and blah.

It doesn't matter the season really. I can forget Jesus in an instant—forget my need for him, forget the truth of who he is, forget what he's done for me and the price he paid in loving me.

I was raised in church and have spent the majority of my life learning about Jesus in Sunday School and reading about him in the Bible. I even went to a Christian college and took classes where he was the main topic of discussion and study. But I think sometimes my overfamiliarity with the stories of Jesus makes me forget him. He becomes more of a flannel graph figure rather than the real-life Jesus I can relate with daily.

When life gets hard and our days feel mundane, when we feel overly-confident in our ability to conquer whatever the world throws at us, or when we grow stagnant in our faith, it's time to encounter Jesus anew. It's time to go back to Scripture, back to prayer, back to diving in deeper, and remember who Jesus is.

Because when we remember who Jesus is, that's when fear takes a hike and our pride crumbles into humility and the mundane is transformed into a great gift.

When we remember who Jesus is, we are put face to face with the truth that faith isn't about performance, but relationship with a living God who sent his Son so that we might live with him—not just in eternity, but here and now.

Over the next 31 days, we're going to take some time to remember Jesus by focusing on his names.

The names of Jesus tell us plainly who he is. They show us how we can relate to him, what he has accomplished, and in some cases, the names of Jesus also define us. So in remembering who Jesus is, we also are reminded of who we are in him.

My hope is that by the end of this study, as we remember who Jesus is, those rough and doubting and hurting places of our hearts get smoothed out as we rediscover this Jesus who is the solid foundation we can stand on, and the one person we can trust to be there no matter our season.

P.S. If you're studying with a group, or if you just want a little extra something for your study, I've got a free leader guide that you can download from my website. Just go to https://jazminnfrank.com/group to fill out the form and then the leader guide will be sent straight to your email! Happy studying!

Bible Study Basics

One of my main goals in every study I create is not to just feed you information and pull lessons out of the passages for you. I want to train you and give you the skills you need to actually study the Bible for yourself.

You'll notice in this study that I will always begin each lesson with the reference to that day's passage and a bit of blank space. Before I ever speak a word about it, I want you encounter the text first for yourself.

I want you to make this study your own. I'm simply here to guide you, give you a few things to think about, and provide a few tools to help you dig deeper into God's Word.

You are perfectly capable of understanding and studying the Bible for yourself. Don't shake your head at me. It's true.

You may not always understand everything you read the first time—or the fifth time—but you can always glean something with the guidance and insight of the Holy Spirit and a few handy Bible study skills.

In these next sections, I'll share a few skills that you will find useful, not only as you move through this study, but in future studies as well.

SKILL #1 BIBLE READING

Each day as you turn to the passage and begin reading, here are a few practices that will help you get the most out of your Bible time. Also, if you're wondering how to use that blank space at the beginning of each lesson, these practices are a great way to utilize that space:

   1. **Start with prayer.** Ask Holy Spirit to help you understand what you read and

reveal important truths you need to hear.

2. Make some observations. Pay attention to what you're reading and take note of what's there.

3. Ask some questions. Is there something there that you don't understand? Ask God about it. Bible reading isn't a passive activity, but an opportunity to engage in conversation with God.

4. Read with a pen in your hand. It might seem scary to write in your Bible or like it isn't allowed, but it is. In fact, marking important words, underlining verses that stick out, or making notes in the margin is a great way to engage with the text.

SKILL #2 CONTEXT

Context is the literary, cultural, and historical setting of the text. Literary context takes into account what other words, verses, and events occur around the passage you are looking at. Cultural and historical context help us understand who the author is, who the text was written for or to, the time period of the text, and what historical events occur around a particular passage.

This kind of information can be found in commentaries or in the notes sections of a study Bible. But since our focus in this study isn't on learning how to navigate these tools, I won't ask you to go hunt it down yourself, but I do want you to be aware of the context of John before we dive in.

The gospel of John was written by John the apostle. He was one of the twelve disciples of Jesus, and one of the three that were closest to Jesus.

This book was written to a mixed audience of Jews and Gentiles sometime toward the end of the first century.

Each gospel writer has a different purpose or angle from which they write their account of Jesus' life and ministry. John is focused on providing the information his readers need so that they will believe that Jesus is the Christ, the Son of God and that in believing, they find life in his name.

In John 20:31 our author states this purpose clearly when he writes, "these are written so that you may believe that Jesus is the Christ, the Son of God, and that by believing you may have life in his name."

Believe and *life* are two words you will find frequently throughout this book. And really these words are the reason we're looking at the names of Jesus in the first place.

Because if you know who Jesus is and what is revealed about him through his names, you can believe that he is exactly who he says he is. And in believing, you find life in him—not just eternal life, but abundant life on this side of heaven too. And that's the goal here—for John in his writing and for us in our studying.

We want to believe and we want to live.

Maybe you picked up this study because something in your heart tugged when you read the description on the back cover. Maybe this is simply the next study in the stack of studies you've been collecting. Maybe you're part of my Devoted Community, or part of another Bible study group and this is the study for this season.

Whatever brought you here, I pray these words, this gospel, these names feed that hunger in you. I pray that they bolster your faith, that they iron out some of the doubts you have about Jesus, and that you are able to trust him more deeply as you remember who he is.

I pray, with John, that you would believe, and in believing you may have life in Jesus' name.

SKILL #3 KEYWORDS

Like I said, I don't want to just hand you information. I want to help you learn how to study the Bible yourself. In this study we'll focus on the skill of marking keywords.

Keywords can be one of two things. They are either words that are used repeatedly in a passage or words that you are specifically looking for. We're going to track both kinds of keywords in this study.

Since belief and life are the main focus of John, I want you to be on lookout for those words and pay attention to how they are used. As you read, keep a pen or highlighter handy and underline every time the words *believe* and *live* (or a variation of those words) are used.

We're also focused on the names of Jesus—names others call him, and those he gives to himself. Whenever you come across a name of Jesus, put a box around it.

Easy peezy lemon squeezey, right?

Underline the words *believe* and *life*. Put a box around the names of Jesus.

Got your pen handy? Then let's get started!

But before we do, let's pray.

Father, you have given us a great gift in your Word. You reveal your heart and make yourself known, and we are grateful that you are a God who wants us to know you. You pursue us and go after us and seek out relationship with us. As we begin this study of the names of Jesus, we ask that you would prepare our hearts to encounter you in a new way. Holy Spirit, give us understanding and wisdom and insight as we read. Help us notice things we've never noticed before. And may we come out on the other end knowing you better and loving you more. May you receive all the glory.

Day 1: Jesus Christ

READ JOHN 1:1-18

Whew! Is your head spinning a little bit? I know mine is.

Whenever I read this first part of the gospel of John, I reel—partly from the beauty of John's writing and partly from the density of this passage. There is just so much info about our beloved Jesus in such a short amount of space.

If you didn't read through the first time with your pen in your hand, go back through and put a box around all the names our author John uses for Jesus.

What names does John call Jesus in these first 18 verses of his gospel?

These opening verses in the gospel of John are rich. So many names.

Word.

Light.

Son.

We'll spend the next few days here, digging into these verses, unearthing the gems. But today we begin our study by looking at the name that is most familiar to us.

Jesus Christ.

This Jesus who was both fully God and fully man came down from heaven and walked the earth in flesh. Though nowadays the name of Jesus is special and sacred, his name back then was actually quite ordinary.

In Hebrew, his name was Yeshua, or Joshua. It was a pretty popular name that meant "savior" or "deliverer." It was the same name of the man who led Israel into the Promised Land after Moses died. You know, the guy named Joshua who was commanded to march around Jericho? And here in the New Testament, that same name is given to God's Son.

Before he was even born, God was clear about what his Son's name would be.

Read Luke 1:26-33 and Matthew 1:18-22. What do these two passages tell us about Jesus and his name?

From the moment the angel declares to Mary that she will give birth to a son, we know exactly who Jesus will be.

Paul declares the importance of Jesus' name in Philippians 2:10-11 when he writes that "at the name of Jesus every knee should bow, in heaven and on earth and under the earth, and every tongue confess that Jesus Christ is Lord, to the glory of God the Father."

God has a special knack for taking what is ordinary and making it holy. The name of Jesus is no different. The name of Jesus is simple. It was popular among the Jews because those sons they named Yeshua carried with them the reminder that one day, in the same way God delivered Israel from Egypt, he would deliver the Jews from their enemies.

The name of Jesus is something special and holy.

It truly is the name above every other name.

We're going to look at a lot of names over the next few weeks, but we're starting here with the name Jesus on purpose. As we move through the rest of this study, I encourage you to hold his name in your heart. Repeat it to yourself over and over.

Jesus…Jesus…Jesus…

Truly there is no sweeter name.

What does the name Jesus mean to you right now?

How do you think knowing the other names of Jesus will help you understand him and be in relationship with him?

Day 2: Word

READ JOHN 1:1-3, 14-18

Right out of the gate John gives Jesus a name that doesn't seem much like a name at all.

Word.

He doesn't even start by saying that Jesus was the word, but in his poetic way he says:

"In the beginning was the Word, and the Word was with God, and the Word was God" (verse 1).

We learn a lot about Jesus from this one verse.

Word here is the Greek word *logos*. You might recognize that name from your English classes in school, or because it sounds very similar to the word logic. The definition of *Logos* is "divine reason implicit in the cosmos, ordering it and giving it form or meaning."[1]

Essentially the name Word means to give something order and form.

By John establishing that Jesus is the Word, he is reminding his readers of the very beginning of Scripture and the beginning of time itself.

With these verses from John 1 in mind, turn back to the beginning of your Bible and read Genesis 1. Underline any instances where you see God giving order or creating form.

Often we see Jesus as only a New Testament figure, but because he was with God and is God from the beginning, we can see Jesus "in the beginning" too. Right from the beginning.

The same God who created the world is the same God introduced in this first verse of John's gospel.

When God spoke the universe into existence, the Word went out and gave things form and meaning. And here in John's gospel, that same Word takes on the form he created. He steps into human flesh and speaks meaning into our lost and dying world.

Jesus is the giver of God's message, and he himself is the Message—God in flesh sent to demonstrate the Father's love.

This is our Jesus. The Word made flesh. Reason and form and order and meaning are all wrapped up in this one name.

Word.

Right from the beginning John establishes that Jesus is God and that he is the revealer of God the Father. Up to this point in history, God had spoken to individuals and made his heart known to one nation—Israel. Now he puts on flesh and dwells among the people he created so that we can see what he is really like; so that we might see his glory.

So that we might be changed as we encounter the Word and allow him to breathe meaning into our lives.

Meaning is the one thing so many of us spend our lives searching for. We want to know our purpose and have significance. John declares Jesus as the answer to that search.

Are you looking for some sort of meaning in your life? You need not look any further than Jesus.

From the very beginning God called you good.

From the very beginning he called you to the work of tending to his creation and he creatively blessed you with passions and gifts to live out that calling in your own unique way.

From the very beginning his desire has been to walk with you, to be in relationship with you, and to show you that all meaning is found in him.

Word is a powerful name of Jesus. It reminds us that Jesus has always existed, and that he had a role in our creation. Indeed, John tells us that "All things were made through him and without him was not any thing made that was made" (verse 3).

The Word became flesh and dwelt among us so we might know that our meaning is found not in our accomplishments, our relationships, our social class, marital status, or income level. No, our meaning and our significance are found in him.

How does knowing Jesus as the Word impact your understanding of him and your relationship with him?

What meaning do you see Jesus giving to your life?

Day 3: True Light

READ JOHN 1:1-13

Do you remember those two words we're marking as we read through John? Believe and live.

John's purpose in writing this gospel is that his reader would believe that Jesus is who he claimed to be—that he is the Son of God—and that we might find life in Jesus.

Both of these words show up powerfully with today's name of Jesus: True Light.

When we first encounter this name in verse 4, light is equated with life: "In him was life, and that life was the light of men."

That statement makes me think of creation. We established yesterday that Jesus the Word was present in the beginning. He played a role, and indeed, he created in the beginning. And the first thing made when God started speaking the universe into being was light.

Light became the foundation of creation, the thing upon which everything else was built: "And God saw that the light was good. And God separated the light from the darkness" (Genesis 1:4).

You may recall from your science lessons and elementary school about how light, specifically sunlight, makes things grow. Flowers and trees all need sunlight in order to thrive.

Even in our natural world we see this truth playing out that light gives life.

The same is true with our Light, Jesus.

Jesus is the Light and in him we find life, both eternal life and abundant life.

This description of Jesus as Light also calls to mind the star of Bethlehem. When Jesus' birth was announced, the star led three wise men from the east straight to him.

Light breaks through the darkness. You can't have darkness anymore when there is light.

Jesus is that light, breaking into the world of darkness and sin and shining with love and grace and truth.

I love what John writes in verse 9: "The true light, which gives light to everyone, was coming into the world" (emphasis mine).

Jesus didn't just come to shine his love on the Jews. He didn't come to eliminate darkness only from Israel.

He came for everyone.

Every single person of every single nationality and background—for everyone who ever has lived and ever will live.

He came for all of us.

But for someone who has spent their whole life in darkness, light can be a disorienting thing. If you've ever come out of a physically dark space into the light of day, you squint and strain to see in the brightness. It hurts a little and you hold your hand up to block the sun as your eyes adjust.

Jesus was disorienting to many people. To the religious leaders he became a blasphemer and a threat to their own comfort and prestige. To many individuals he encountered, Jesus shook up their way of life in a truly uncomfortable fashion.

He was fully God, yet fully man, and the world didn't know him. The nation that had been gifted with generations of prophecies about the coming Messiah did not recognize him when he showed up on the scene (verse 11).

Jesus knew this coming in. He knew people wouldn't believe him and that they would seek to snuff out the true light. Yet still he pursued them. And as their spiritual eyes adjusted, they came to recognize Jesus for who he is—the True Light who came into the world to break the bondage of darkness.

The True Light who came to give new life in the glow of his love and grace.

The True Light who welcomes all who believe into the family of God.

Read verses 12-13 again. What privilege is given to those who believe in the True Light?

With Jesus as our light, we have no need to fear the darkness. It will never overtake him. In fact, he has already put darkness in its place.

This image of Jesus as the True Light is one we can experience now, but it is one we will experience in a deeper way in the future.

Our author John also wrote Revelation. This book is an account of a vision John had later in life when God revealed to him how this world would pass away and New Jerusalem would come.

Toward the end of Revelation, he shares this revelation about the holy city:

> "No longer will there be anything accursed, but the throne of God and of the Lamb will be in it, and his servants will worship him. They will see his face, and his name will be on their foreheads. And night will be no more. *They will need no light of lamp or sun, for the Lord God will be their light,* and they will reign forever and ever" (Revelation 22:3-5, emphasis mine).

The Lord *is* the light and the Lord *will be* our light.

Praise be to our God who has not left us in darkness but gave us the True Light to live by. Sin and death no longer have a claim on us because Jesus our True Light has overcome that darkness.

How does knowing Jesus as Light impact your understanding of him and your relationship with him?

In what ways do you need Jesus to shine his light into your life right now?

Day 4: Lamb of God

READ JOHN 1:19-37

Today our author John introduces us to another John—John the Baptist. When this John was approached and questioned about his identity, he made it very clear who he was. He himself was not the Prophet or Elijah, but a voice in the wilderness preparing the way for the one Israel had been waiting for. He was a forerunner heralding the coming of one who was greater than himself.

It is John the Baptist who declares the name of Jesus we will focus on today.

In verse 29, the day after John the Baptist is questioned, Jesus shows up and John names him immediately: "Behold, the Lamb of God, who takes away the sin of the world!"

What a strange name. At least in the gospel of John, this is the first name Jesus is given publicaly. Lamb of God.

What does that name mean to you right now? Why might John the Baptist call Jesus the Lamb of God?

For the other Jews standing nearby who heard John speak, the immediate image this name would have conjured up were the lambs sacrificed at the temple. Jewish law required the sacrifice of unblemished lambs to cover the sins of the people. The priests performed these sacrifices daily on behalf of Israel.

Read Exodus 29:38-46. What was the purpose of these daily sacrifices?

Every day the priests offered two lambs, one in the morning and one in the evening, an offering to God as a pleasing aroma, an act of worship and obedience, and a daily reminder that it is the Lord who makes the people holy.

The entire sacrificial system, with its various details about when and how to perform different sacrifices throughout the year, was to remind the people of their need for God—to remind them that apart from him they can never be holy. He pursued humanity first and made a way for relationship to be restored between us and him, and the cost was the blood of a lamb.

But the Old Testament sacrifices were just a shadow of things to come.

Read Hebrews 10:11-18. Why is the name Lamb of God so fitting for Jesus based on this passage?

Jesus did something the priests could never do. He atoned for our sin once and for all. We don't show up at the temple with our spotless lambs anymore because the Lamb has already been slain. His blood was shed, his skin torn, his body broken, his blood poured out for the forgiveness of sins.

Once and for all.

Jesus is our perfect and spotless Lamb. And here in the first chapter of John's gospel, John the Baptist makes the declaration of Jesus' name. *Behold the Lamb of God.* Because he is the one who takes away the sins of the world.

How does knowing Jesus as the Lamb of God impact your understanding of him and your relationship with him?

Take some time to write out a prayer of thanks to Jesus for his sacrifice.

Day 5: Rabbi

READ JOHN 1:35-51

Yesterday we read about John the Baptist's declaration about Jesus. On a first read of verse 29, it seems John is just openly speaking the words, "Behold, the Lamb of God who takes away the sin of the world!" I tend to picture him standing near the Jordan River where he has been baptizing. People are milling about, and when he notices Jesus he makes this declaration.

But today's passage sheds some light on a few specific people who were with John the Baptist when he declared Jesus' name as the Lamb of God.

According to verse 35, who is with John the Baptist?

As you read, did you notice that little word "again" tucked in there so quietly?

"The next day *again* John was standing with two of his disciples…"

This tells us that these two disciples—one we know is Andrew, and the other is unnamed, but could be our author John—were there yesterday to hear the Baptist's declarations about Jesus. Perhaps, since they were disciples of John the Baptist, they were there to witness Jesus' baptism.

Read about Jesus' baptism in Mark 1:9-11. What would have made that experience so memorable?

Regardless of what these two disciples saw, we do know what they heard. The teacher they had been learning from, John the Baptist, made some incredible declarations. They'd been with him long enough to hear what he was preaching, though no one yet knew what this Messiah looked like.

Read Luke 3:1-17. What were some of the main points John the Baptist was preaching?

These disciples were hearing all of this. So when Jesus shows up that second day, and for the second time John the Baptist points to Jesus and declares, "Behold the Lamb of God," Andrew and the unnamed disciple follow. They had heard enough about Jesus from the Baptist and they were curious enough to follow him.

Jesus, in his classic form, notices the two men and asks them, "What are you seeking?" Essentially it's a "What do you want?" or "What are you expecting?" kind of question. Jesus' question isn't rude but invitational as he opens the floor for Andrew and the other disciple to voice their intentions.

The men reply, "Rabbi (teacher), where are you staying?" On first read this seems like an odd response. Perhaps they got nervous in Jesus' presence and that was the first thing they thought of. But students of that time period often stayed pretty close to their rabbis and perhaps this was their way of asking Jesus to let them be his disciples.[2]

When the men call Jesus "Rabbi" and make the choice to follow him, it's like they are saying, "We've heard a lot about you, Jesus, and we're ready to learn from you. Make us your students."

That's all a disciple is, a student. One who sits at the feet of a teacher and learns from him.

And that's one way Jesus invites us to relate to him—as disciples.

Jesus' time as Rabbi didn't end with his time on earth. Through the Holy Spirit, Jesus is still teaching us today how to love and live in his grace and how to help others know him. He still offers that "come and see" invitation to us, inviting us into deeper intimacy with him, always having more to teach us about himself.

How does knowing Jesus as Rabbi impact your understanding of him and your relationship with him?

What have you learned from Rabbi Jesus recently?

Day 6: Son of God

READ JOHN 1:14-18, 29-34, 43-51

One thing you'll notice as we continue to move through John is that a lot of the names we're exploring in this first chapter (yup, we are still only in chapter 1!) will be repeated and used throughout the rest of this gospel. "Son of God" is one we'll see a lot.

Just in chapter one alone we've seen it three times.

Write down the three verses where "Son of God" or "Son of the Father" is used in chapter 1.

What do these verses reveal about Jesus?

Our gospel writer uses the name "Son from the Father" in verse 14. John the Baptist calls Jesus the Son of God in verse 34, as he recounts the experience of baptizing Jesus. And Nathanael calls Jesus by the same name when Jesus reveals that he saw Nathanael under the fig tree before Nathanael ever came anywhere near Jesus.

This name is a powerful one, and it's one that ties directly into John's purpose in writing this gospel.

Do you remember what that purpose is?

So that you may believe and live...

John is writing this account so that we might believe Jesus is exactly who he says he is.

As we move deeper into this gospel, we will see Jesus making some really outlandish claims that God is his Father, he is God's Son, and that together they are one. But right from this opening chapter John wants to make it clear, before Jesus himself says anything, that what Jesus says is true.

He *is* the Son of God.

He is perfectly human and fully God. He is divine. And that's what makes his names worth studying. Because if he isn't God, he's just some quirky teacher making outrageous claims. He's a liar or a lunatic at best. What he teaches is hard and a little bit crazy, and there is no way I would follow him if it weren't for this essential piece of his identity: that he is the Son of God, a member of the Trinity, fully and completely God.

He always has been and always will be.

Up to this point we've heard little from Jesus. He offered the invitation to a few disciples to "Come and see" and revealed the knowledge he had of Nathanael before the two stood in the same space.

But all of the names we've explored so far have been spoken about him. Our author has given us several of them and John the Baptist contributed a couple, as did the first disciples.

Now as we move into chapter two, Jesus is going to become more active and more vocal.

If you've been putting boxes around the names of Jesus, you might also know that we've skipped a couple, but don't worry. We'll circle back around to them. Names like Messiah, Son of Man, and King of Israel will show up again and we'll dig deeper into those names then.

But here in chapter one John's laid out a good foundation for us.

Jesus is....

The Word

Light

The Lamb of God

Rabbi

The Son of God

He is divine and perfect, sinless and loving, gracious and true.

Jesus is worthy of your trust.

How does knowing Jesus as the Son of God impact your understanding of him and your relationship with him?

Of the names we've looked at so far, which one has been the most meaningful for you and why?

Day 7: Sovereign

READ JOHN 2:1-12

Throughout John's gospel, you might notice that some of the names we pay attention to aren't explicitly in the text. When I taught middle school English, one of the skills we taught our students was how to uncover what the author was saying when it wasn't stated plainly. If the author doesn't clearly say the sky is blue, what information from the text lets us know this is true?

Some of the names of Jesus work this way too.

John doesn't plainly tell us that Jesus is sovereign—and perhaps this is more an attribute than a name—but it is there all the same, shown through the story of Jesus' first miracle.

I love this story. First because Jesus is at a party. Sometimes when we've been in church too long, we can create this image of a God who is stern and serious all the time, and I just don't believe that's true. As humans, we're created in the image of God, which means we share his attributes. He put things in us that he has, and I believe the ability to laugh and have fun is one of those things.

Creation itself tells me God had fun making this world. Look at the pomegranate or the ostrich or how clouds aren't just white fluff in the sky, but can appear in different shapes.

The fact that Jesus is at a wedding shouldn't surprise us. Jesus knows how to have fun.

So Jesus, his disciples, and his mother, Mary, are all there together for this wedding feast. But then the wine runs out—which will put a damper on any party—and Mary volunteers Jesus to come up with a solution. She knows who he is. She remembers well the message from the angel that she would give birth to the Son of God (Luke 1:30-33).

Though Jesus' ministry hasn't begun yet, Mary knows what Jesus is capable of. She knows that he can take a nothing situation and make something out of it.

And that's exactly what Jesus does.

He asks some servants to fill some large jars with water, and then to fill a cup and take it to the host of the party. With just a word, water become wine, and not just decent wine or good enough wine, but the best wine (verse 10).

This element that had been created by the Word was transformed into something abundantly good.

To be sovereign means to rule with absolute authority. There is no one higher or more in charge. Everyone and everything obeys the whim and rule of the sovereign ruler. And here at a simple wedding feast, we see Jesus stepping into that role.

He is sovereign.

Remember, one of the things John is trying to convince us of is that Jesus is God. He is the Word who is with God and is God, and it has been this way from the beginning. He is the Son of God, God in flesh, walking around the very world he created. And he rules it all. Not with an iron fist or an unkind hand, but in love. He is good and giving and kind and everything is under his care.

It is after this first miracle at a wedding in Cana that his disciples first believe (verse 11).

This first miracle, this first show of Jesus' sovereignty, isn't showy or spectacular. He did it quietly, but news of this miracle spread quickly. Jesus, the carpenter's son, had made something ordinary into something extraordinary.

And the people begin to wonder if, perhaps, there is more to this Jesus guy than they first thought.

How does knowing that Jesus is sovereign impact your understanding of him and your relationship with him?

In what ways do you need Jesus to show his sovereignty—his absolute authority—over your life right now?

Day 8: Temple

READ JOHN 2:13-25

The temple was the place the Jews would go to meet with God and offer their sacrifices. It was the place of worship and the place of encounter and was the focal point of the Jewish faith.

When God first led Israel out of slavery in Egypt, part of the Law he gave them through Moses was instructions for how to build the Tabernacle, which was like a mobile temple. It was the place where the priests served and where God's presence dwelt.

Generations later, King Solomon built a permanent house for the Lord, not that God was confined to the walls of the temple. Instead, both the tabernacle and the temple symbolized God's presence among his people.

With this in mind, what do you think is the significance of Jesus referring to his body as the temple?

At the time this event occurs, Jesus is in Jerusalem for the Passover. His public ministry has begun. He is teaching and people are starting to recognize his name. Yet when he comes to the temple and finds stalls of animals meant for sacrifices and salesmen who have jacked up the prices to make a profit off the Jews in town for the feast, Jesus gets angry.

The people have forgotten the purpose of the temple. The people have forgotten what it looks like to view the Lord and his house with a heart like David's.

Read Psalm 84. What are David's thoughts about the house of God?

Jesus is furious and heartbroken that the people have made the temple into something it was never meant to be.

But those people were there on business. They probably made good money during Passover, and they questioned Jesus about his actions.

"What sign do you show us for doing these things?"

Jesus answers, "Destroy this temple, and in three days I will raise it up" (John 2:18-19).

The people of course missed the point because Jesus was talking figuratively. Our author clears that up for us though, explaining that Jesus "was speaking about the temple of his body" (verse 21).

In two years' time, Jesus will be back in this city, back for this same celebration to remember the time when God led his people out of slavery, and at that time in a matter of three days, Jesus' body will be torn down and built back up. He will be crucified and then raised to new life; and anyone who chooses to believe in him is raised to new life through Jesus. Through Jesus, we are freed from the slavery of sin and our relationship with the Father is restored.

Jesus is our temple. He is the One who makes it possible to step into the presence of the Father. He is our meeting place with God.

How does the image of Jesus as the Temple impact your understanding of him and your relationship with him?

How will you meet with Jesus today?

Day 9: Son of Man

READ JOHN 3:1-36

Sometimes this passage feels a little disjointed and hard for me to follow. It's one of the most widely referenced passages in sermons about salvation, but when I read it, sometimes it feels like Nicodemus and Jesus are talking on two completely different levels. Which I guess they are. Nicodemus sees the physical, but Jesus is trying to get him to see the spiritual so that he might believe.

Nicodemus was a Pharisee. Pharisees were the religious rulers in Jerusalem at the time. They were often the ones Jesus spoke to and rebuked because, while they kept the letter of the Law, they did not understand the heart behind it. They believed following the rules was what made them holy, when it reality, it was a heart seeking to know God. When we allow *him* to make us clean and new, that is what makes us holy.

Nicodemus was different from the other Pharisees, though. Instead of trying to shut Jesus up, he was curious and invited him into conversation.

As Jesus started making his way around Jerusalem, it was obvious that he was not your average teacher. He was doing things, as Nicodemus pointed out, that no one can do unless God is with him (verse 2). Many called Jesus "Rabbi" and affirmed that he was a good teacher, but Nicodemus seems convinced that there is more going on here.

In an effort to learn more, Nicodemus meets up with Jesus once night has fallen. He addresses Jesus as Rabbi, a sign of respect coming from a religious leader who was trained to do his job, when Jesus had no formal training. Nicodemus situates himself at Jesus' feet as a student, ready to learn.

"Truly, truly, I say to you, unless one is born again he cannot see the kingdom of God" (John 3:3).

Jesus responds to Nicodemus's observation that Jesus' signs and miracles are proof that God is on his side by pointing him right back to the kingdom of God. This born-again language would confuse someone outside of the Church today just as much as it confuses Nicodemus, because physically, it's impossible. Once a person has come out of the womb, they cannot go back in and be reborn (and all the mommas shout hallelujah!).

But Jesus isn't addressing something physical here. He's talking about the spiritual.

Reread verses 5-8. What is required to be born again?

This statement goes back to what John the Baptist said when he pointed to Jesus as the one who would baptize with the Holy Spirit.

Jesus himself is the Living Water, and he is the one who baptizes with the Holy Spirit (John 1:29-34). This rebirth that Jesus is talking about is spiritual, not physical.

But Nicodemus struggles with this. How can this be?

This is where Jesus moves from talking only about the kingdom to talking about himself—how he is the one to usher in this kingdom as the Son of Man, perfectly human, yet perfectly divine.

To illustrate his point, Jesus points Nicodemus back to Moses and the serpent.

Read Numbers 21:4-9. How does this story point to what we know about Jesus and what he came to accomplish?

In the same way the people of Israel believed what God said and looked up at that serpent on the staff and were healed, Jesus is telling Nicodemus, "I am like that serpent on the staff in the wilderness. I have come to heal people and restore them and make them new. Whoever turns their eyes toward me and believes will be saved and will have new life."

Despite what the religious leaders taught, salvation wasn't something that could be earned through works. They couldn't do enough, wash enough, or sacrifice enough to be completely clean from their sin.

It simply came down to belief.

It came down to turning their eyes to the Son of Man and believing that he is the new-life giver. He is the one who can bring our hearts to the point of rebirth.

Jesus offers that same invitation to us. *Look at me. Trust me. Believe me. And I will make you new.*

In what ways is Jesus making you new?

How does the image of Jesus as the Son of Man impact your understanding of him and your relationship with him?

Day 10: Savior of the World

READ JOHN 4:1-45

Any time Jesus interacts with a woman, I tend to perk up and pay attention. He's always so gentle and kind. This was unusual in the Jewish world. While Jewish women were generally treated better than women in other cultures, there was still an expectation that women did not matter as much as the men. Foreign women had even less value, so the fact that Jesus takes the time to talk with a Samaritan woman is pretty counter-cultural.

And if her heritage and gender aren't bad enough, we are also quick to learn that this woman Jesus strikes up a conversation with also has a reputation. She's had five husbands and currently lives with a man she is not married to. That's why she is fetching water from the well during the hottest part of the day, so she can avoid the other women.

This woman is an outcast in all meanings of the word, yet Jesus takes the time to talk with her.

In fact, it seems this meeting at the well is a divine appointment, not just for this woman, but for the whole town.

Jesus' conversation with the woman at the well is chock-full of things we could pick apart and dissect and apply, but what we're most interested in unearthing in this study are the names of Jesus.

Remember, it's in knowing the names of Jesus that we are reminded of who he is. That's our goal here—to know Jesus better.

The name we discover here is declared by the townspeople as a result of the woman's testimony. After Jesus tells her everything she has ever done and reveals himself as Messiah (verse 26), she goes and tells the rest of the town. The outcast becomes the evangelist: "Come, see a man who told me all that I ever did. Can this be the Christ?" (verse 29).

As our author John explains, Samaritans and Jews didn't have many dealings with each other. Samaritans were not full-bred Jews, but had a mix of Jewish and Gentile heritage. Still, pieces of Jewish culture and beliefs remained, including the belief that Messiah was coming as the prophets foretold. The woman's testimony about Jesus was convincing enough that the people went to him and asked him to stay. And as he taught them, they began to believe.

Reread John 4:39-42. Describe the progression of the people's faith. What made them believe?

The woman's testimony served as an invitation to Jesus. The people believed what she said and they went to hear more and meet this Jesus for themselves. Once they did, they came to the life-changing conclusion that Jesus wasn't just a prophet or the Jewish Messiah. He was the Savior of the world (verse 42).

Jesus spends most of his ministry teaching and healing and ministering to his own people, yet here on this little side trip through Samaria, these people get it. Jesus came for everyone. His salvation is for the entire world.

How wonderful that must have been the day the people believed—the day they realized they weren't excluded anymore. They weren't considered other-than. Instead, they saw Jesus' salvation for them, too.

It's for us, too—for us non-Jews who weren't blood-born into Israel's family, yet are born again as children of Abraham when we choose to believe Jesus and receive him as our Savior.

How marvelous, how wonderful is the love and intentionality of Jesus. He seeks out any and all who are far from him. He desires relationship. He desires that none shall perish, but have everlasting life with him (John 3:16).

How did you come to believe Jesus? Did he reveal himself directly to you, as he did the woman at the well? Or did someone else's testimony draw you near enough to meet Jesus for yourself?

How does the image of Jesus as the Savior of the world impact your understanding of him and your relationship with him?

Day 11: Healer

READ JOHN 4:46-5:17

At the end of chapter four and beginning of John 5 we find two events of Jesus healing. The name "healer" isn't explicitly assigned to Jesus here. In John 5:11 the formerly lame man refers to Jesus as "the man who healed me," but no one directly calls him "Healer."

In the first event, Jesus is coming into town—back to the place where he performed his first miracle and turned water into wine—when an official approaches him and asks Jesus to heal his son.

After the wedding miracle, it seems word has spread. The people have heard what Jesus can do and one official has sought Jesus out to heal his dying son.

Look back at the text. How does Jesus respond to the official's request?

John is once again highlighting this theme of belief. *Unless there is a sign, you won't believe.* In some ways, Jesus' statement comes across as a challenge. People have heard about the wedding miracle, and perhaps news has been carried from other places about what he has taught and the other things he has done that no normal man can do. There's something different and even novel about him.

Jesus is well aware that some people just hang around to see the next cool thing he can do, and in his response to this father, he challenges the people on this point. *Don't just come to watch the show. None of this matters if you don't believe.*

In many instances throughout the gospels, however, these signs and miracles are exactly what lead people into faith, and this official is one of them.

He pleads with Jesus, "Sir, come down before my child dies," and Jesus assures the man that his son will live. The man believes and hurries home.

John draws attention to the man's belief a second time when a servant meets the official on the road and gives news that the child is improving. And again, the man believes, perhaps at an even deeper level. Because while he believed Jesus' words enough to go home and wait for his son to be made better, perhaps he expected a slower, more natural healing process. The fact that the boy started improving at the very same moment Jesus said "the boy will live" heightens the man's belief.

The words of Jesus have power to heal at a distance and to heal in an instant.

Jesus is Healer.

In this first event, Jesus is approached by someone asking for healing, but in the second one Jesus approaches the lame man by the pool and asks him if he wants to be healed.

What is the man's response to Jesus question?

Two different scenarios, two different ways Jesus interacts with these men, but both receive healing. One asks for it. One is invited into it. Both experience Jesus in a profound and life-changing way and believe. Their lives are different because of the words Jesus spoke.

"Your son will live."

"Get up, take up your mat, and walk."

The man at the pool expects healing to come if he can just get to the water. Instead, Jesus speaks and the man stands. And even more than that, when Jesus shows up again later, he invites the man into an even deeper healing.

"Sin no more..."

The man's legs are healed, but Jesus wants to bring an even deeper healing to the man's soul.

Allow yourself to come face to face with the Healer today.

What healing words do you need to hear from Jesus today? What healing are you asking him for? What kind of healing is he inviting you in to? Ask him to reveal himself to you as Healer and trust the way he chooses to heal you.

How does the image of Jesus as Healer impact your understanding of him and your relationship with him?

Day 12: Son

READ JOHN 5:14-47

Perhaps when you saw the title of today's lesson, you scrunched up your eyebrows and flipped back a few pages. *Didn't we already talk about Jesus as Son already?* Yes, yes, we did. But as is the case with God's living and active word (Hebrews 4:12), there are always more layers to explore, more things to understand, a deeper way to know our Lord.

Today we cycle a little deeper into who Jesus is as Son.

In this passage Jesus uses both Son of God and Son of Man to describe himself.

What does Jesus say about himself and his relationship with the Father? (There's a lot here; just jot down a few of the things that stuck out most to you.)

Let me back up a little bit and set the stage. This passage is part of the same conversation Jesus is having with a group of religious leaders in Jerusalem after he heals the man by the pool. The miracle happened on the Sabbath and the leaders are grumbling about that.

In Jewish culture, Sabbath was one of the big laws everyone adhered to. Six days of work, one of rest.

The heart behind this law was that the people would trust God's provision and believe that he would take care of them as he promised. However, the leaders of Jesus' day wanted to be extra holy, so they tacked on a few extra stipulations of their own about what you could and could not do on the Sabbath. Apparently the healed man carrying his mat and Jesus doing the work of healing were not acceptable Sabbath practices.

That's their first issue with Jesus. But the second is even more problematic in Jewish beliefs.

Go back to the beginning of today's passage. What other issue do the religious leaders take with Jesus?

According the Merriam-Webster, blasphemy is the act of insulting or showing disrespect for God, or claiming the attributes of deity.[3] If Jesus were merely human, this would be a huge issue. But he isn't.

Jesus is exactly who he says he is.

He is Lord of the Sabbath. His Father is always working, and now so is he, and the work both seek to accomplish is to bring people back into thriving relationship with the Triune God.

But the religious leaders have missed the point and Jesus calls them out on it.

Reread verses 39-47. What is Jesus' main issue with the religious leaders?

It all comes back to that word doesn't it?

Believe.

Believe that Jesus is who he says he is.

Believe that he was sent by the Father.

Believe that his goal is relationship and that we might have eternal life through him.

Believe that he is the fulfillment of every promise made in the Old Testament.

Believe that he is the Son of God.

Where is your belief? What do you believe about Jesus? Is there anything in this passage that is challenging for you? Take some time in prayer and share your thoughts, doubts, and questions with the Lord.

How does this deeper knowledge of Jesus as the Son impact your understanding of him and your relationship with him?

Day 13: Bread

READ JOHN 6:1-71

This passage humors me in some ways and really challenges me in others.

The feeding of the five thousand is one of those well-known miracles of Jesus. He takes a boy's small lunch, gives thanks, and multiplies the food to feed a multitude with leftovers to spare. The group eats their fill and the next morning goes back in search of Jesus, only to find that he has gone to the other side of the sea, so they get in their boats and follow.

When they get there, Jesus immediately gets to the heart of the issue. "Truly, truly, I say to you, you are seeking me, not because you saw signs, but because you ate your fill of the loaves" (verse 26).

He knows why they came—to see a cool miracle and to get their bellies filled once more. But he cautions them that there is more to this life than a full belly. He challenges them to start paying attention to spiritual things.

And this is the part that makes me laugh a little, the way these people respond to Jesus' rebuke. They ask what they need to do in order to do God's work, to which Jesus responds that all they need do is believe in him.

"Then what sign do you do, that we may see and believe you? What work do you perform? Our fathers ate the manna in the wilderness; as it is written, 'He gave them bread from heaven to eat.'" (verses 30-31).

Our ancestors got bread and believed in God's provision, so, yeah, you should totally do that for us, too. Then we'll believe.

But Jesus being Jesus uses the moment to teach them about spiritual things.

You guys want to talk about bread. Awesome. Let's talk bread. I am the bread.

Jesus takes something so completely ordinary and mundane and turns it into an object lesson. He is the true bread, the bread of life, the living bread. He is the one who satisfies and fills and sustains.

Yes, God provided manna for Israel during their years in the wilderness. Each morning the bread appeared with the dew, and the people gathered what they needed that day, ate, and were satisfied. In the same way, Jesus invites us to come and eat of him. Not in a literal sense, but a spiritual one.

Think about the Lord's Supper, about the bread and the wine and what they mean. Each time we take and eat and drink, we are receiving grace and declaring our trust in him—our need for him.

That's the same thing Jesus invites the people into here. *Eat of me,* he says. *Trust me. Seek me daily. Step out of your tents and receive this bread from heaven—bread that gives eternal life. Bread that sustains you and satisfies you on a soul level, to the deepest parts of you.*

For many of the people listening to Jesus that day, his teaching was hard because, though he was offering them his flesh to eat metaphorically, they took him literally. They came seeking literal bread, but Jesus offered himself as spiritual bread and they just didn't get it.

What was the crowd's ultimate response to Jesus' teaching about the bread?

Then Jesus turns to the twelve.

Describe the interaction between Jesus and Peter in verses 66-71.

Not everyone who heard Jesus speak that day rejected his words. The twelve disciples believed. They had seen the water changed to wine. They had seen Jesus heal people who had spent their whole lives sick and in physical pain. They had heard him teach. And perhaps they understood something in Jesus' teaching about the bread that the rest of the crowd did not.

They believed, and the fact that they stayed was an act of receiving that bread. They trusted Jesus. They genuinely believed him. And later on, when Jesus and his disciples sit in that upper room and Jesus offers them the bread and the wine, maybe some of them remember this moment; they remember Jesus' words about the bread. They remember that *he* is the bread.

How does the image of Jesus the Bread impact your understanding of him and your relationship with him?

In what ways do you need to "eat of Jesus" today? What do you need from him today and what is he seeking to give you?

Day 14: Christ

READ JOHN 7:1-52

This is definitely not the first time we see this name. In the very first chapter, our author calls him Jesus Christ, the giver of grace and truth (John 1:17).

Let's do a little word study here. If you've been marking the names of Jesus as you read, this will be super easy. Flip back through the first six chapters of John and jot down anywhere the name "Christ" is used. Also make note of the context—who is using that name and why.

The name Christ (or Messiah) means "anointed one."

For the Jews it would have conjured up images of their kings who were anointed. Anointing was the act of taking oil and pouring it over the head of someone God had chosen for a specific purpose.

When Israel demanded a king, God let the people have what they wanted and instructed the prophet Samuel to anoint a man named Saul (1 Samuel 10). After a few years, Saul's heart began to harden toward the Lord, so God instructed Samuel to go out to Bethlehem and anoint a shepherd boy named David to be the next king (1 Samuel 16).

Being anointed was a sign that a person was chosen by God to lead. The people expected the Christ the prophets wrote about to be their next king, another David. But Jesus was a king of a different sort. He would not sit on an earthly throne to rule a geographic nation. Instead, he would bring his kingdom to earth and invite any and all who believe to enter in and be a part of that kingdom.

The gospel of Luke shares an account of a time early in Jesus' ministry when he stood up and read a passage from Isaiah.

Read Luke 4:16-21. According to this passage, what was Jesus anointed to do?

Jesus came to rule and reign in a way the people did not expect. And that was part of what caused so much division. Some people looked at the signs he was doing and believed. *This Jesus from Nazareth is definitely the Christ!*

Others looked at him and crossed their arms. *Surely this isn't Messiah. This isn't the Christ. He wouldn't be breaking the Sabbath, but keeping it. He wouldn't come from Galilee, and especially not Nazareth. He wouldn't be stirring up so much trouble. No, this guy isn't at all what we expected the Christ to be, and he can't possibly be it.*

But isn't that so often how Jesus comes? He seems to like showing up and shaking up people's view of him. Remember that Samaritan woman at the well? The fact that he showed up and struck up a conversation with her was quite jarring. No upstanding Jewish man would speak to her, but Jesus did.

As we continue to move through the rest of John, we'll see Jesus upsetting the apple cart, talking to people law-abiding Jews would not talk to, touching people who were considered unclean, giving grace where the letter of the law demanded consequence.

All the while living into his purpose in coming—to set the captives free and bind up what has been broken and to declare the year of the Lord's favor.

Jesus is the long expected Christ, embodied in an unexpected way. Who would have thought that God himself would come down in flesh and walk among the very people he created? Who would have thought that the ruler of the universe would not demand a golden throne, but instead walk the dusty roads and eat with sinners and touch those considered unclean?

To all those people hearing Jesus and asking, "Can this be the Christ?" yes, he is. He may not be the Christ we expected, but he is the Christ we needed.

How does knowing Jesus as Christ impact your understanding of him and your relationship with him?

In what ways has Jesus surpassed your expectations or done something unexpected in your own life?

Day 15: I AM

READ JOHN 7:53-8:59

There is a lot going on in this passage. A woman receives mercy and grace. Jesus declares himself the light of the world, and the people he is speaking to refuse to believe what he is saying.

The people stick around and argue with Jesus' bold declarations until he tosses out the name we're focusing on today: I AM.

In context for us English readers, when Jesus says in verse 58, "Truly, truly, I say to you, before Abraham was, I am," the sentence feels awkward and incomplete. First of all, you're mixing your tenses, Jesus. Abraham was, I am? That's not right.

Grammatically, this sentence is very wrong, but Jesus is saying exactly what he means.

Sometimes I'll read that "I am" part and a few of those ellipses run through my head. You are........what, Jesus? Finish your sentence, man!

But he did.

Jesus said exactly what he meant, and the Jews understand and reach for the nearest rock to stone him because they've heard that I AM name before. They know the claim he is making here.

Flip back in your Bible to the Old Testament for a moment and let's read Exodus 3:1-14.

How is the I AM name used here? Why do you think the Jews in our John passage get so riled up about Jesus using that name for himself?

I AM is the personal name for God—Yahweh. This name is a reminder of God's Godness, his faithfulness, how he always has existed and always will exist, how he is creator and sustainer of life.

And this is the name Jesus is claiming.

"Before Abraham, I am."

Abraham had lived a couple thousand years before Jesus walked the earth and was considered the father of Israel. He was the patriarch of their nation, and Jesus is not only declaring that he existed during the time of Abraham, but before him. Jesus is clearly claiming divinity here. If his previous points about the bread and the light and being Lord of the Sabbath didn't get through, this point does.

The people hear it loud and clear and won't receive it. King, Prophet, Teacher. Sure, we can handle those names. Bread was a little weird, but the disciples got on board with that one. But this one? This I AM name? That's going too far.

And it would be. If it weren't true. But it is.

Jesus is I AM.

He is the God of the universe. He is the Word and Light and Bread. He is the sustainer of all life, the giver of grace, the revealer of truth.

He is God. And when we accept that, all the other names we've already studied and the ones we'll look at in the days ahead all gain a little more weight. Jesus isn't just a good teacher or a prophet. He isn't some lunatic claiming that he is bread. He is the God of the universe, the Creator of all things. He is the one who called Abraham, the one who spoke to Moses through a flaming bush, the one who spoke to Samuel, the one who wrestled Jacob.

Jesus is the Alpha and Omega, the Beginning and End. Everything that ever has existed and ever will exist finds its life and breath and meaning in him.

How does knowing Jesus as I AM impact your understanding of him and your relationship with him?

Finish the I AM statement below as if Jesus was writing you a note to remind you of who he is. What do you need to remember about who he is today?

I AM...

Day 16: Light of the World

READ JOHN 9:1-41

Today Jesus and his disciples are on the move again, and as they're traveling, they come upon a man who is blind. The disciples ask Jesus whose fault the man's blindness is. Is the man blind because he sinned or because his parents sinned?

To us as modern day readers, the question sounds ridiculous. We attribute this kind of condition to the body just not functioning as it should; but in the ancient Jewish world, physical ailments and suffering, like blindness, were thought to be punishments from God for some act of disobedience of that person or someone in their family.

Jesus addresses this question clearly.

According to Jesus, what is the reason for this man's blindness?

Sometimes suffering isn't a result of sin but an opportunity for God's glory to be revealed through us and to us. That was the case for this man. His blindness, though he'd lived with it all his life, is about to collide with the glory of God.

It is here in this man's physical darkness that Jesus reveals himself as the Light of the World.

This is a name we've already studied back in chapter one, a name John attributed to Jesus. But here Jesus says it about himself.

There is something really satisfying about how Jesus reveals himself as the Light of the World to a man who has lived his entire life in darkness. It's basically the best object lesson, and I can only imagine what it meant to the man who was healed from his blindness.

Do you notice the progression? At first the man simply calls him by his given name: "The man called Jesus." Then when the Jewish leaders ask him who the man thinks

Jesus is, he replies that Jesus is a prophet. But as the back and forth continues and the religious leaders are trying to convince the man that there is no way that Jesus is from God because he doesn't keep the Sabbath, the man is adamant. No one who was born blind has ever regained their sight. That's never happened before. He makes the point that since God doesn't listen to sinners, Jesus must be sent by God.

Skim back through verses 8-38. Make note of the different ways the formerly blind man refers to Jesus.

Do you notice the progression? At first the man simply calls him by his given name: "The man called Jesus." Then when the Jewish leaders ask him who the man thinks Jesus is, he replies that Jesus is a prophet. But as the back and forth continues and the religious leaders are trying to convince the man that there is no way that Jesus is from God because he doesn't keep the Sabbath, the man is adamant that someone who is born blind and gains his sight has never happened before, and God doesn't listen to sinners. So obviously Jesus is from God.

That angers the leaders, so they kick him out, and when the man runs into Jesus again, we see the second layer of God's glory being revealed. We see another layer of what it means for Jesus to be the Light of the World.

This isn't just about a man physically seeing light. Jesus isn't just a light-giver. He is the Light. And in this second conversation with Jesus, the man confesses his belief and calls Jesus Lord and worships him.

Not only have his eyes seen the daylight, his soul has encountered the Light of the World—the One who gives life. The One who breaks through the darkness. The One who gives light to everyone (John 1:5-8). His light doesn't shine only on the Jews or the righteous or the perfect or those who have it all together. Nope. His light shines on everyone, across the world and across the generations, illuminating those barriers keeping us from him and inviting us to step into his warming, life-giving light.

In what ways do you need Jesus' light to shine on and in your life right now?

How does encountering Jesus again as the Light of the World impact your understanding of him and your relationship with him?

Day 17: Good Shepherd

READ JOHN 10:1-42

The same men who were in conversation with Jesus yesterday after they threw the man healed of blindness out of the synagogue are the same men Jesus is addressing in our passage today as their discussion turns toward sheep.

In classic Jesus fashion, he begins by speaking figuratively about thieves climbing into the sheep pen, and how only those who enter by the door are the shepherds the sheep trust. Sheep, while they are not the brightest animal, do know the voice of those who tend to them and will follow their shepherd because they trust him and recognize his voice.

This discussion sets things up for Jesus to reveal another one of his names: Good Shepherd.

Now, you might be thinking, "Wait a second. Doesn't he call himself the door, too?"

Why yes, he does. Great observation!

And this is where my Bible nerd-ness starts to come out a bit. When we read "I am the door," we picture a physical door or gate. However, often in those times the shepherd himself would lay in the opening of the sheepfold—which would have been something like a courtyard penned off by a stone wall. The shepherd physically became the door. If anything wanted to get in to harm the sheep, it had to go through him first.

So by saying he is the door, Jesus is making himself the protective barrier between the sheep and the thief who comes to steal, kill, and destroy.

Jesus is the protector, caretaker, and provider of the sheep (and we're his sheep).

Read Psalm 23. How does this familiar passage come to life when you read it knowing that Jesus calls himself the Good Shepherd?

Now read Psalm 139: 1-14. Part of what makes Jesus a Good Shepherd is that he knows us. Every detail about us. What details about his knowledge of you are most comforting from this psalm?

There is one more detail that makes Jesus a Good Shepherd, and that is his inclusion.

Jesus states that he lays his life down for the sheep, and not just the Jewish sheep: "And I have other sheep that are not of this fold. I must bring them also, and they will listen to my voice. So there will be one flock, one shepherd. For this reason the Father loves me, because I lay down my life that I may take it up again" (verses 14-17).

One of the recurring themes in John is his inclusion of both Jews and Gentiles in God's salvation mission. Everyone is invited into the fold, and anyone can enter through the blood and sacrifice of Jesus.

He is the door.

He is the Good Shepherd.

He is the One willingly laying down his life to take it up again so we can be raised to new life through him.

As his sheep, we don't have to worry about being cared for or knowing where we're headed. We can simply trust our Good Shepherd to lead and provide.

We can trust his protection.

We can trust him to lead us to places of peaceful rest and to walk with us through the dark valleys of life. There is no need to fear what this life holds because Jesus is with us.

Always.

How does knowing Jesus as the Good Shepherd impact your understanding of him and your relationship with him?

How is Jesus shepherding you right now? Are you currently in a season of peaceful rest, or does life look more like a valley? Take some time to recommit yourself to the Shepherd's care and declare your trust in him.

Day 18: Resurrection & Life

READ JOHN 11:1-44

Remember that question the disciples asked Jesus about the man born blind when they encountered him on the road? "Lord, whose fault is it that this man was born blind?"

What was Jesus' response to that question?

So that the glory of God would be revealed.

In John 11 we read of another situation that accomplishes this same purpose, where God's glory is revealed.

Lazarus, brother of the famed Mary and Martha, and close friend of Jesus, has fallen ill. Word is sent to Jesus, but because he loves this family, Jesus stays where he is for two extra days.

Every time I read that verse I always stop. *Wait, what? If you loved someone that much, wouldn't you get to them as fast as possible? I know if a close friend of mine were really sick, I'd be throwing some essentials in a bag and going to them right away.*

Yet Jesus choosing to stay two extra days is declared an act of love. He explains it to his disciples when they finally set out for Bethany. "Lazarus has died, and for your sake I am glad that I was not there, *so that you may believe.*" (verse 14).

Jesus knows what will happen when he gets to Bethany. He knows he will encounter mourners, and he knows he's going to perform his greatest miracle yet and raise Lazarus back to life. And all of this for the sake of belief.

So that his disciples and Mary and Martha and all the people at the tomb will know that he is God and he has authority over death.

Once they arrive in Bethany, Jesus doesn't even make it into town before Martha comes running out to meet him. This same Martha who is lovingly corrected in Luke 9 for being distracted by so many things meets Jesus while he is still on the road and declares boldly, "Lord, if you had been here, my brother would not have died. But even now I know that whatever you ask from God, God will give you" (verse 21-22).

Martha believes that Jesus is who he has been saying he is. But she also knows the world she lives in. Once things have died, they do not rise again. Not in this age, anyway. Resurrection is a later thing. So when Jesus tells Martha, "Your brother will rise again," Martha nods and affirms his statement. "I know that he will rise again in the resurrection on the last day" (23-24).

But Jesus is talking about something more. He's talking about a now-thing, not a later-thing.

"I am the resurrection and the life. Whoever believes in me, though he die, yet shall he live, and everyone who lives and believes in me shall never die" (verse 25-26).

Resurrection is coming, but also, resurrection is here because Jesus himself is the Resurrection and the Life. He is the one who raises us up from the deadness of sin and restores us to new life and relationship with him. Though our physical bodies will die, our souls will not. And when the end of this age does come, we will be given new bodies.

In Jesus the old is made new, the dead is raised back to life, and that life isn't just a better version of the old—it is something completely new.

When Jesus raises Lazarus and restores him to his sisters, this is just the beginning of Jesus' resurrecting power. For in just a little while, Jesus himself will face death. He will lie in a grave. And he will rise again, conquering sin and death and showing the world that what he said to Martha is true.

He is the Resurrection and the Life.

How does knowing Jesus as the Resurrection and the Life impact your understanding of him and your relationship with him?

What things in your life have died that you want to see Jesus resurrect? These could be dreams, passions, habits, relationships, desires. Whatever it is, share that with him. And maybe ask him about what he wants to resurrect in you too.

Day 19: Anointed King

READ JOHN 11:45-12:19

Jesus has been shaking things up for a while now. Ever since he showed up on the scene, he's had a reputation for messing with the status quo and upsetting the religious leaders. Now Jesus has gone beyond simply healing on the Sabbath and has raised a man back to life who had been dead for four days. People believe in Jesus now, and the Pharisees are starting to become afraid.

Passover is quickly approaching and Jesus and his disciples show up in Bethany again. While having dinner, Mary sets aside her position as servant and host and she lowers herself to her familiar place at Jesus' feet. Cracking open an expensive bottle of perfume, she begins to pour it over his feet, anointing him.

We talked about what it means to be anointed in an earlier lesson. Do you remember what it means?

When Mary anoints Jesus' feet it is an act of devotion, love, humility, and preparation.

Read the account of this same event in Matthew 26:6-13. What else do we learn about Mary's act from Matthew's account?

Jesus' feet and his head were anointed. It's an act of worship, yes. An act of preparation for Jesus' death. But I also can't help but see reflections of the Old Testament anointing here. When someone or something was set apart for God's purposes—mostly priests, kings, and sacred elements in the temple—they had oil poured over them.

And here we have Jesus who, after being anointed, rides into Jerusalem like a king on inauguration day. He is mounted on a donkey with the people lining the road, waving palm branches, and calling out, "Hosanna! Blessed is he who comes in the name of the Lord, even the King of Israel!" (verse 12:13).

A lot of the discussion in John's gospel so far about Jesus has been focused around whether or not Jesus is the Christ, the chosen one of God, the anointed one who was promised to save his people. Israel expected a military leader to kick out their Roman oppressors. Instead they got someone greater.

They got a King who went to war against the enemy of their souls and came out victorious. The Anointed One sent by God to save his people not from a physical empire, but to reign forever, not as the ruler of Israel, but as King in the kingdom of God. This kingdom is not bound by time or geographic barriers and it is not limited to a certain ethnicity of people. Citizenship in this kingdom is offered to all of us who believe.

Jesus is King. King of the universe. And King of our hearts if we let him.

Today, and every day, let's come to the feet of Jesus as Mary did. Let's crack open our hearts and offer up a fragrant aroma of worship and praise and devotion.

This is our King. And he deserves to be honored. Whatever we have, let's pour it out as a willing offering.

How does knowing Jesus as the Anointed King impact your understanding of him and your relationship with him?

What do you have today that you can offer to Jesus as a gift and act of worship? It doesn't need to be a physical item. Sing him a song, express words of praise, or simply offer your heart. Take some time to do that now.

Day 20: Light

READ JOHN 12:20-50

I said at the beginning of this study that some of these names of Jesus we would tackle more than once, but maybe it's surprising to you that we've landed back on Light again. I know it surprises me. I've read the gospel of John numerous times and never have I been so aware of just how much of a theme light is here.

So let's recap what we know about Jesus as Light so far:

> Jesus is the True Light that breaks through the darkness.
>
> Jesus is the Light of the World, and his light gives life to everyone.
>
> His light illuminates those barriers keeping us from relationship with him and invites us into deeper intimacy.

If life is the goal of John, light is the continual beacon pointing us toward the life that comes when we believe.

As you read through today's passage, what new things did you notice about Jesus as the Light?

As I read, I kept imagining this image of a lighthouse. Jesus is describing himself as the Light who draws people to himself, the Light that points people back to the Father. Isn't that just what a lighthouse does? It serves as a beacon for ships, drawing them to land and directing them to safety.

Jesus is like a lighthouse.

But there is another layer of this whole light theme that gets unearthed here. Look again at verse 36: "While you have the light, believe in the light, *that you may become sons of light*" (emphasis mine).

Light isn't just a core piece of Jesus' identity, but when we believe—when we step into the light and receive relationship with him—we become sons and daughters of the Light. We become little lighthouses too, shining into the dark choppy waters of this world and drawing lost life-sailors to shore, to safety, to the arms of a loving Father who has done everything to get them back.

For those people listening to Jesus as he spoke in Jerusalem, just days before he would be lifted up on a cross and crucified, he was trying to get them to understand, trying to get them to see the life-giving Light right in front of them.

Paul writes to Timothy years later that God "desires all people to be saved and to come to the knowledge of the truth" (1 Timothy 2:4). We see that heart through Jesus' words here.

Come. Believe. Step into the light. You don't have to remain in darkness anymore. Come.

And that is always his invitation. Like the sweeping light of a lighthouse set up on a hill, Jesus is constantly shining, constantly beckoning the lost and worn out and weary to come near, to come home and rest in the safety, security, and freedom of the Light.

How does knowing Jesus as the Light impact your understanding of him and your relationship with him?

How can you shine Jesus' light to someone you encounter today?

Day 21: Servant

READ JOHN 13:1-20

Do you remember what Jesus told Nathanael when Jesus revealed that he had seen Nathanael under the fig tree before they ever met? He said, "Greater things than this you will see." The disciples have seen a lot of amazing things.

These men have been with Jesus for three years now. They've listened to him teach and they've believed what he has said. They have stuck by him when others deserted him, and they have learned to place their trust in him.

They have seen Jesus heal blind eyes and lift the lame to stand on strengthened legs. They've seen him feed thousands of people with one sack lunch. They've seen him cure the incurable and welcome those who were traditionally unwelcomed into his space. They've seen him even raise the dead.

Yet here, on this Passover night, in an upper room in Jerusalem, they see him do something they never expected—Jesus acting as a servant as he kneels to wash their feet. This man they have spent the last year calling Teacher and Lord now claims the role of a servant.

And I wonder if seeing Jesus stripped down to a servant's level of dress and kneeling before their dirty feet might be one of the greatest sights they've seen. And by great, I mean completely earth-shaking.

I mean, he's Jesus. The Christ. The One who has come to set his people free. He should be the last person washing feet. Yet here he is, toting a bowl of water and a towel around the room as he washes the feet of his disciples.

What does this image of Jesus washing feet do to you? What do you think about Jesus here in this moment?

Things go smoothly until Jesus gets to Peter. Perhaps everyone else is so in shock or so humbled at the sight that they don't know what to say or do. But Peter never seems to be short on words.

Describe Jesus' interaction with Peter. Why do you think Peter takes such issue with Jesus washing his feet?

Like any good teacher, Jesus models for his students what he expects of them.

Love well. Serve well. Follow my example: "For I have given you an example, that you also should do just as I have done to you" (verse 15).

In Matthew 20:26-28, we see Jesus presenting this message another way: "But whoever would be great among you must be your servant, and whoever would be first among you must be your slave, even as the Son of Man came not to be served but to serve, and to give his life as a ransom for many."

When we want to remember Jesus, normally we remember him for his grace and sacrifice, his forgiveness and love. Rarely do we recall that he made himself a servant. Because when we do, we're bound to remember that living as a servant is what he expects of us too.

That's not to say that we live based on performance and that the more we do for people the more highly Jesus will think of us. No, it's the heart of the matter.

Jesus made himself a servant to show others their value in the kingdom of God. He bent low to wash dirty feet because that act of service did something for his disciples. It became a symbol of the way he cleanses us from everything that keeps us from living in right relationship with him. And his dialogue with Peter is a reminder that even when we have been washed clean and forgiven of our sin, there are still areas of our life Jesus wants to work with us on as he continues to make us more like him.

Living as a servant doesn't mean you live with the belief that your life and your needs matter any less than someone else. Rather it means living in a constant state of loving others more than yourself, loving them sacrificially in a way that points them to the God who sacrificed so much for them.

Today take some time to sit quietly as the disciples did. Whether in awe, shock, or humility—or all of the above—let Jesus wash and make clean that corner he's been asking to work on with you. Allow him to be your model of what service looks like, then turn to those around you and follow his example.

How does knowing Jesus as a servant impact your understanding of him and your relationship with him?

How are you currently living as a servant? What have you believed previously about what it means to serve as Jesus did? In what ways does today's lesson affirm or shake up those beliefs?

What areas in your life is Jesus asking you to let him wash, clean, purify, and sanctify? Take some time to offer that to the Lord and invite him to do his cleansing work there.

Day 22: Way, Truth, Life

READ JOHN 13:21-14:31

If there is one thing Jesus has been trying to get his disciples to understand, it's that he and the Father are one, and that because the disciples have seen and known Jesus, they know the Father too. Because while the Father and Son are distinct members of the Trinity, they are both part of the same God who has always existed.

Here in these final hours he has remaining with his disciples, Jesus is trying to let them in on what's about to happen. He's about to go away and he will not be with them any longer. He's speaking of heaven and being in the presence of the Father. And in much the same way we respond when we try to wrap our heads around the ways of the Trinity, the disciples are confused.

What question does Thomas voice in verse 5?

It's this question that sheds light on another name of Jesus. Or rather, three names: Way, Truth, and Life.

You want know how to get to where I'm going, Thomas? I am the way.

Jesus has already said that he's going to the Father and the only way to the Father is through Jesus Christ. He is our mediator and our go between. He is the one who cleanses us and makes it possible for us to relate to the Father. He is the lighthouse always drawing us nearer to himself and pointing us to the Father.

He is the Truth.

From the beginning of time the Word existed, and the Word is Truth. Jesus has delivered many true statements during his ministry and the truth has always been that he is God. That is what he wants his disciples to believe. That truth is what gives them life.

"Do you not believe that I am in the Father and the Father is in me? The words that

I say to you I do not speak on my own authority, but the Father who dwells in me does his works. Believe me that I am in the Father and the Father is in me, or else believe on account of the works themselves" (John 14:10-11).

This is the very thing our author John has been drawing attention to this whole time.

Jesus isn't some great teacher or prophet, though those names are attributed to him. He's more than that. He is the Son of God, the very likeness of the Father, God in flesh, Immanuel, God with us.

He is also Life. We saw this statement come up in our lessons about how Jesus is the light and that light gives life.

The commandments he has given aren't commands meant to hinder our lives, but to help us live our *best* lives. He is the creator of life and he knows how this world best functions.

But Jesus doesn't just give life. He *is* Life. "Because I live, you also will live" (verse 19b). It's John 3:16 all over again—anyone who believes in him will not die, but will live. Forever. Though our bodies perish, our souls are safe to spend eternity with him because of his work on the cross.

Way.

Truth.

Life.

Jesus is all three. And when we get hold of that, when we remember these names, we remember just how secure we are in him. He has everything we need. He *is* everything we need.

How does knowing Jesus as Way, Truth, and Life impact your understanding of him and your relationship with him?

Which of these three names do you most need to remember today? What is Jesus reminding you about him through that name?

Day 23: True Vine

READ JOHN 15:1-17

This section of John 15 might be my favorite passage in all of Scripture. I turn to it often when I need to remember who Jesus is and who I am in him.

He is the Vine. He is the source. All of our worth and purpose and love and grace come through him. It is through Jesus that we know and can live out our calling. It is in him that we know our identity as children of God.

And when we're invested in cultivating that relationship that is when we thrive.

Jesus is the True Vine and he names his disciples—that's them then and us now—the branches.

How beneficial is a branch without a vine?

Without its source of nutrition and growth, a branch is nothing. It has no way to bear fruit. It is stagnant and dead, good only for stoking a fire or maybe building a house of sticks (and the Three Little Pigs showed us how well that turned out).

Jesus says that our job is to just stay attached.

Abide is the word he uses. To abide simply means to remain. To stay. To dwell with.

Another word I use often for this is to live devoted—to be committed, faithful, and steadfast in your relationship with Jesus.

Abiding in Jesus requires both rest and commitment. We rest in the truth of who Jesus is, and we remember him as the Word and Light and Vine and all the other names we've explored in this study. We simply sit with him and let him be the Lord of our life.

We live committed to him. No matter what season we're in or what our circumstances look like, we've made the decision that we're sticking with him.

Through thick and thin, good and bad, in joy and sadness—we're with Jesus. We're letting ourselves be found in him. We're spending our time with him. We're seeking him and allowing ourselves to be pursued by him.

Knowing Jesus as the Vine takes some of the pressure off because it's not about making sure I check off all the boxes and dot all the i's so he loves me.

Knowing Jesus as the True Vine and abiding in him means I just stay. I show up and I make space for him in my life. I let him *be* my life.

And as we do that—as we abide—we bear fruit. When we abide, Jesus' life works through us and we are able to pour out love and grace to others.

How does knowing Jesus as the True Vine impact what you understand about him and how you relate with him?

In what ways can you abide in Jesus the Vine today?

Day 24: Overcomer

READ JOHN 15:18-16:33

"But take heart; I have overcome the world" (John 16:33b).

How often do we flip to this verse when life has gotten hard? How often do we need a reminder that this Jesus we serve and love is the one who overcomes?

This message we are so quick to flip to in times of trouble is the message Jesus leaves his disciples with.

The hours are ticking away. Judas left a while ago to fetch the guards who would arrest Jesus, and here in the evening hours after Passover dinner, Jesus is wrapping up his final lesson.

This lesson comes with a warning that the world will hate those who are faithful to Jesus. They hate because they do not know, but that hatred will lead to the persecution and suffering of Jesus' disciples.

He tells them this to warn them, to prepare them for what's ahead. But he doesn't leave them only with the "you're going to suffer" message. Instead, he redeems that suffering with the assurance that he has overcome the world.

I like that Jesus makes this statement before he goes to the cross. Right now it doesn't look like he's done much. Sure, he's performed miracles and gathered quite a following, but that's not exactly "overcoming the world" kind of stuff. And in a few hours Jesus will hang on a cross, bloodied and beaten, and that most certainly doesn't look like overcoming. That looks like defeat. That looks like the end.

But we know resurrection Sunday is coming. We know how this story really ends.

And so does Jesus. It is for this purpose that he came.

So before the cross and before the resurrection, Jesus makes his statement: "I have overcome the world."

It is already a done deal. There is no question about that. And because he has overcome, we have joy.

Have you noticed how often in these last couple chapters of John that Jesus has used the phrase "that your joy may be full" or "your joy made complete"?

Joy is what Jesus wants for us.

When we make the choice to believe, he asks us to abide, and as we abide in him we find joy in his presence.

Read Psalm 16:5-11. What does joy look like according to this passage and how do we get it?

Joy is knowing that no matter what, Jesus is there and he's always for us and with us. He fills us up and gives us opportunities to pour out his love to others. He is our strength in hard situations, our wisdom and our truth when the rest of the world seems to be caving in. He is our confidence, the steadfast, steady, immoveable rock on which we stand.

Joy is something we can carry simultaneously with sorrow, and it is not determined by our circumstances. It is supplied by the Vine in which we abide.

Jesus overcame so that we might find joy in him—complete joy, full joy, abundant joy.

Rest in the presence of your Overcomer today. Abide in him and may you be filled to overflowing with a soul-level joy.

How does knowing Jesus as Overcomer impact your understanding of him and your relationship with him?

How are you claiming joy today? In what ways do you see Jesus staying near and overcoming on your behalf?

Day 25: High Priest

READ JOHN 17:1-26

The name of Jesus we're focused on today isn't actually stated in the text itself, but if you take a look at the heading for this chapter, depending on your translation, you'll probably find some sort of variation of that name there.

Write down the heading in your Bible for this chapter here:

In Jewish Law, the High Priest was head over all the other priests and had special duties he performed. One of those duties required that he go once a year into the Holy of Holies—that portion of the temple where the ark of the covenant was kept—and present an offering there.

The High Priest acted as a go-between for God and the people of Israel. He was the one responsible for presenting the sacrifice that provided atonement for the sins of the people and, because he too was a sinful human, that sacrifice atoned for his sins, too.

Jesus is the perfect High Priest. This is one of the main images of Jesus presented in the book of Hebrews.

Read Hebrews 4:14-5:10. What does this passage teach us about Jesus as high priest?

The role of the High Priest was to intercede, or to pray on behalf of the people. Here in John 17, we see Jesus doing just that.

Look back at the following verses in today's reading and summarize what Jesus prays for in each passage:

Verses 1-5

Verses 6-19

Verses 20-26

He prays for his disciples and even for himself, but something that might surprise you is that he prays for you too. Did you catch that?

When Jesus prays for future believers, he's praying for you and me who believed because of the testimony and teaching of his disciples. Those original 11 told people about Jesus who told people about Jesus who told people about Jesus, and somewhere down the line we heard and believed.

How do you feel knowing that Jesus prayed for you?

Jesus intercedes on your behalf, asking that the Father would make himself known to you and that his love would fill you.

That's crazy amazing stuff. And I don't know about you, but it grounds me. It sets my feet solidly on the fact that Jesus wanted me with him then just as much as he does now. Just as he wants all of us with him. Every single human in history.

Jesus is the great High Priest, acting as our go-between, making a way for us to be in relationship with God. He is on our side, eager for us to know the Father.

How does knowing Jesus as High Priest impact your understanding of him and your relationship with him?

In what ways is it a comfort knowing that Jesus is your High Priest?

Day 26: King of the Jews

READ JOHN 18:1-19:22

And now we reach the part of the gospels where I get quiet and read a little slower.

We've spent the last twenty-five days reading about Jesus, studying his names, remembering who he is. We know who he is and we have come to believe. And now, here we are. This Jesus who is the Way, Truth, Life, Word, Vine, and King has been arrested and accused, and now he's hanging there on that cross.

This is what the prophets wrote about and the entire Old Testament kept pointing to—how Messiah would come and save his people from their sins. His people meaning not only the Jews, but all of humanity. And that salvation would come through the spilling of blood and the death of our Lord.

In those final hours before his hands and feet are nailed to the cross beams, when he stands before Pilate, the Roman governor, another name is bestowed on him: King of the Jews.

Jesus had been brought to Pilate early in the morning. The sun has recently risen and the Jewish leaders are already heated. They want Jesus dead, and Pilate is the man who will be able to carry out the death sentence they desire.

"Are you the King of the Jews?" Pilate asks in the privacy of his quarters.

What is Jesus' reply?

It's as if Jesus is asking Pilate what he believes. *Do you believe I am the King of the Jews or is that what others have told you?* But Pilate sidesteps the question. He isn't concerned with beliefs here. Rather he wants to finish this business and get on with his day.

Pilate knows the religious leaders are angry with this man before him, angry enough to demand he be crucified, but he can't find a reason. So he tries to release Jesus, but the people demand the release of local criminal Barabbas instead. Jesus is to be crucified.

Pilate over and over again refers to Jesus as the King of the Jews and even writes it on a sign that is nailed above Jesus' head on the cross. When the religious leaders take issue with it, Pilate answers, "What I have written I have written" (verse 22).

But Jesus isn't King of the Jews. Originally that's what the people wanted—a king trained in battle and ready to gather an army to overturn Rome. But he isn't that. He is a much higher King.

When he is being questioned by Pilate, Jesus tells the governor about his kingdom. Look again at verses 18: 36-37. What does Jesus say about his kingdom?

*The kingdom Jesus is speaking about is a heavenly one and it's the same one Jesus has been teaching about from the beginning of his ministry. It's the same one he's been inviting people into. All they need to do to enter into this kingdom is believe.

This name assigned to Jesus—King of the Jews—is one of mocking and uncertainty. It's a place holder because the people, the leaders, and Pilate can't accept the truth.

Jesus isn't just King of the Jews. He is King. Period. King of our hearts, King over our lives, King of this universe that he spoke into being. Yet here is the King, beaten, tortured, mocked, humiliated, stripped, and nailed. And all of it was for us—for you.

Read Isaiah 53:4-6. Based on this passage, what did our King accomplish on that cross?

The mark of a good king is the care and concern he has for his people, and Jesus is the greatest King this world has ever seen. Not a King of the Jews, but King of all who believe in him.

What does it mean to you that Jesus is King?

Have you allowed Jesus to be King of your life? How do you see him fulfilling that role?

Day 27: Fulfillment

READ JOHN 19:23-42

One of the handiest tools when studying the Bible is to pay attention to repeated words or phrases within a particular book or passage. It's why we're marking the various names of Jesus and making note of just how many times the gospel of John uses the words "believe" and "live."

Because when you pay attention to what's repeated, you can start to see what the author really wants us to understand.

Today's name comes out of a phrase that's repeated multiple times in our passage: "that the Scripture might be fulfilled."

Go back to the passage and underline every time you see that phrase or a variation of that phrase.

How many times did you find it in the passage?

Look at each instance this phrase is used and the context immediately surrounding it. According to the passage, what is being fulfilled in Jesus' death?

Now this is where Bible study gets fun. Because our passage is referencing other passages, and when we take time to visit those other passages, they can shed some more light and understanding on our focus passage.

So are you ready to go on a bit of a scavenger hunt? Take your pen with you and let's see if we can find those verses our author John is referencing.

The first time John refers to the Scripture being fulfilled is in verse 24 when the Roman soldiers who crucified him are casting lots for Jesus' clothes.

Turn to Psalm 22. It's a bit of a longer psalm, but I want you to read all of it. Read it with the crucifixion in mind. How does Jesus fulfill what is in this psalm?

Crazy right? That psalm was written by David generations earlier, yet we see Jesus so clearly there. Those words were about him. And here in John 19 we see them fulfilled.

But that is not the only scripture fulfilled in Jesus.

Read Psalm 34:15-22. How do you see Jesus here?

And one more. Zechariah 12:7-10. How is Jesus the fulfillment of this passage?

Are you freaking out in the best possible way like I am? Our passage in John today is sad and depressing, and whenever I put myself into the shoes of Jesus' disciples and picture looking on this man I believed to be Messiah hanging on the cross, I feel utterly hopeless.

But the beauty of being on our side of the story is we know what's coming. And we have the rest of the Bible to point back to and say, "All those passages prophesying about the coming of Messiah and the salvation he would bring, God did it. God really did do what he said he would do."

Jesus is our answer.

Jesus is the fulfillment of all those words, even down to the smallest details like his clothing not being torn and his bones not being broken. God is a detail-oriented God and he spoke those details generations before Jesus walked the earth so that when those words were fulfilled in him, we would know beyond a shadow of a doubt that this was all God.

It is mind blowing and soul filling. This was all planned. None of this was accidental, but fully intentional.

How does knowing Jesus as the Fulfillment impact your understanding of him and your relationship with him?

What was your biggest takeaway from today's lesson?

Day 28: Lord

READ JOHN 20:1-18

I want you to imagine that day. Allow your emotions to get involved. Close your eyes to picture it if you need to. Give your heart permission to go there, to be there that morning, walking with the women to the tomb. You saw Jesus on that cross three days ago, you heard him cry out, you saw him breathe his last, and you felt the earth quake.

The men had already taken Jesus' body to the tomb, but because of the Sabbath you weren't able to prepare his body. The waiting was agony. You wanted to do something, you had to do something, but all you could do was rest until this morning, when you gathered your herbs and spices and set out for the tomb.

When you arrive, your heart leaps into your throat then drops to the pit of your stomach because the tomb is open. The rock has been moved aside. You rush with the others to make sure Jesus is still there, but he isn't. It doesn't make sense. None of it makes sense.

But it's in those places of confusion that God's light shines brightest and shows up in unexpected ways.

It is here where we see the three-days-dead Jesus resurrected. He is alive and well, and it's nothing quite like we ever imagined.

How does it feel to know that he's alive? That he conquered death?

Later you hear Mary Magdalene's story. About how she saw him. She saw Jesus standing before her. He called her by name. And she called him Lord.

Did you notice that in our passage? How Mary repeatedly calls Jesus Lord?

The word she uses in Greek is *kyrios*—master, sovereign, the one who has the power to make decisions. It is a name of honor and respect and submission.

Mary Magdalene had entrusted her life and her heart to Jesus. Perhaps that's why she's the first to see him. She was all in. She believed. It was why she was so grieved to find Jesus' body missing, and so overjoyed when she realized he was alive again.

This name perhaps has the most weight in how we relate with Jesus because in naming him Lord, it places us in submission to him. It means we're giving him the power to make decisions and decide what our lives will look like. It means we give up control of what we want and follow where he leads us.

This name is hard because when we choose to call Jesus Lord, it means things change. They have to. We can no longer stay where we are, instead we are invited to move forward with Jesus as our leader and guide. We don't become his puppets, but we do become faithful servants, serving as he taught us how. And we become children, our belief in his lordship gifting us the adoption into God's family.

Life changes when we call Jesus Lord.

Have you encountered Jesus as Lord? Have you assigned that name to him in your own life? Take some time now and ask Jesus to be Lord of your life. Tell him what that means to you. Allow it to change you. And then listen to what your Lord has to say. Invite him to speak and call you by name as he called Mary.

Day 29: My Lord... My God

READ JOHN 20:19-29

Jesus is alive! News has spread among the disciples, though Mary Magdalene is the only one to have seen the resurrected Jesus. No one quite knows what to make of it. Everyone sits gathered together in the same space, afraid to go outside, afraid of what the people might do to them after what was done to Jesus.

And suddenly he's there. Jesus is there, standing in the room. He hadn't climbed through a window, and there was no way he could have entered through the locked door. He's just simply there.

"Peace be with you," he says.

I can imagine peace is what they needed in that moment on multiple levels. They're hiding, they're scared, and the man they saw dead and buried three days earlier is now standing before them alive and well. I'd be needing a healthy dose of peace, too.

What else does Jesus do to calm their fears?

Standing in the room with his wounds and scars exposed, the disciples believe and are glad. Their Lord is not dead. He's alive! And not only is he alive, but here in this space he commissions them and breathes the Holy Spirit into them, just as he breathed life into Adam in the beginning.

But there is one disciple who misses this reunion.

What did Thomas say he needed before he would believe Jesus was alive?

And what did Jesus do?

You know what I love about this encounter with Thomas? It's the fact that Jesus shows up. Just like he taught about the lost coin, the lost sheep, and the lost son (Luke 15), Jesus is always willing to show up for one person. Just one.

The other disciples had already seen, already believed, but Thomas needed something extra. He needed a personal encounter with his risen Lord. He didn't just need to see Jesus; he needed to touch him in order to believe.

And Jesus answered that desire. He held out his hands and said, "Put your finger here, and see my hands and put out your hand, and place it in my side. Do not disbelieve, but believe" (verse 27).

Believe.

That overarching theme we've been talking about.

Believe that I am who I say I am.

Believe that I am alive and I am here and I showed up for you, Thomas.

And he shows up for you, too.

In the midst of unbelief and doubt, Jesus shows up. Locked doors and doubting hearts and the desire for proof don't scare him away. He is willing to show up for the one who is struggling and doubting and needing a sign. And when Thomas did see Jesus, he fell on his knees in worship: "My Lord and my God."

Thomas, like the others, had seen Jesus do a lot. They believed that he was Messiah. Jesus' appearance here three days after he was crucified is further proof that he isn't just the savior sent from God. He is God.

And not a distant God or a far off God, but the God who comes near. The God who desires intimate and personal relationship with each and every one of us. The God who will do anything to reach us.

Thomas doubted. That's what we know him for—his moment of doubt when all the other disciples stood firm in their belief. But Jesus didn't leave him in that doubt. He showed up and Thomas made the bold declaration of his now unshakeable faith.

"My Lord and my God."

Jesus is Lord and God.

Not just the Lord and God of the other disciples.

But Thomas's Lord and God.

Doubting is simply an invitation for deeper faith. It's an opportunity for us to make a request and ask Jesus to show up in a physical way that takes our doubt and turns it into unshakeable faith.

Jesus always comes for the doubting. He always shows up for the one who wants to believe but just needs a little something extra like Thomas.

How does calling Jesus "My Lord and My God" impact your understanding of him and your relationship with him?

Are there any ways in which you doubt as Thomas did? What would you need from Jesus in order to believe? It's okay to ask him to prove himself. He did it for Thomas. He can do it for you, too.

Day 30: Redeemer & Restorer

READ JOHN 21:1-25

Since the resurrection, we've seen Jesus appear to his disciples and show up for the sake of individuals. In this encounter by the sea, though other disciples are present, I believe Jesus shows up for Peter. This is a divine appointment.

Peter, a fisherman by trade before he became a disciple, decides to go fishing and some of his friends and fellow disciples join him. They spend a night on the sea doing what he knows best, but when dawn comes, their nets are still empty.

And that's when Jesus shows up.

The funny thing about this encounter is that it feels so very familiar to another one between Jesus and Peter at the very beginning of Jesus' ministry.

Read Luke 5:1-11. What is similar and what is different between Jesus' encounter with Peter in Luke and the encounter in John?

It wasn't too long ago that Peter stood by as Jesus was being tried by the high priest and Peter denied three times that he even knew Jesus. I can't imagine what that must have felt like—this man who had sworn he would die right beside Jesus couldn't even admit that he knew the man. I'm certain shame crept in and his heart broke. He had denied the man he called Master and Teacher and Messiah.

Yet Jesus doesn't cast him off. Instead, Jesus shows up for Peter and the circumstances feel oddly familiar to how they first met. It's like Jesus is giving Peter a do-over, or even better, a fresh start.

This encounter is all about redeeming and restoring what had been lost the night Jesus was arrested.

Look again at the dialogue between Jesus and Peter in verses 15-19. Do you notice what Jesus is doing here?

Three times Peter denies Jesus. And three times Jesus asks if Peter loves him. One statement of love to cover each denial.

That is grace if I've ever seen it.

Instead of keeping Peter at arm's length and denying him as Peter had denied Jesus, Jesus comes close and offers a clean slate.

Here on the beach, after everything that's happened between Peter and Jesus, Jesus offers the invitation again, just as he did when he first called Peter to be his disciple. "Follow me." And suddenly it's like Peter has come full circle.

In that one statement Jesus gives grace and forgiveness. He restores Peter to right relationship and is essentially saying, "Let's move forward from here together."

There is nothing the Lord can't restore. There isn't a person Jesus cannot redeem. That's his business, after all. It's why he came. Because we all like sheep have gone astray. We've wandered away from our Good Shepherd. We chose darkness over the Light. We drowned out the Word. But Jesus can restore and redeem anything and anyone.

That is grace.

That is our Jesus.

How does knowing Jesus as Redeemer and Restorer impact your understanding of him and your relationship with him?

Is there anything in your life that needs redeemed or restored? Have you strayed away from the Lord? Confess that here and ask Jesus to give you a do over, a clean slate, a fresh start.

Take some extra time here and express your love for Jesus as Peter did. Tell him what he means to you.

Day 31: My Jesus

For the last 30 days you've immersed yourself in the names of Jesus, and you've read the entire gospel of John! That's a big deal. And it deserves some time for remembering and reflecting.

The questions below are meant to guide you through some personal reflection. Use it as a time of prayer and meditation to meet with the Lord in a bit of a different way.

Describe where you were mentally, emotionally, physically, and spiritually when you began this study. What was happening? What made you pick up this study? What were you hoping to get out of it?

NAME ABOVE ALL NAMES

Each name of Jesus we've studied is listed below. Beside each name write one sentence to declare your faith in Jesus using each of his names:

Jesus Christ

Word

True Light

Lamb of God

Rabbi

Son of God

Sovereign

Temple

Son of Man

Savior of the World

Healer

Son

Bread

Christ

I AM

Light of the World

Good Shepherd

Resurrection and the Life

Anointed King

Light

Servant

Way, Truth, Life

True Vine

Overcomer

High Priest

King of the Jews

Fulfillment

Lord

My Lord...My God

Redeemer and Restorer

What was the most impactful name you studied during the last 30 days?

What do you know about Jesus now that you didn't know before?

What were you reminded of about Jesus that you had forgotten?

What's your big takeaway? What is one thing from this study you are going to apply to your life?

How are things different now than when you started this study? What has changed? What's the same?

What's next? Now that this study is over, what is the next thing you want to study or next way you sense God inviting you to encounter him?

One last note...

Thank you so much for joining me in this study of the names of Jesus through the gospel of John. I hope that through the pages of this study you've come to know Jesus better, that your faith has been encouraged, that you have remembered and believe him, and that in him you are finding abundant life.

I also hope that you learned a few Bible study strategies that you can take with you into your own personal study of God's Word.

Before we leave this space I wanted to invite you to keep in touch. You'll find me regularly on Facebook and Instagram as @jazminnfrank. You can also connect with me on jazminnfrank.com, where I've got a slew of helpful blog posts and resources on all things Bible study, navigating your faith journey, and living freely as God's child. This is also where you can sign up for my weekly email devotional and the #10daydevochallege to help you connect with God in new ways.

If you want to keep growing in your study skills and study the Bible with a group, I lead the Devoted Community Facebook group. Each week I provide some teaching on a Bible-related topic and a few conversation starters to build community (you can find a link to that group on my website).

It's been a real joy to journey with you through this study.

May God bless you and keep you as you leave this place. May he cause his face to shine upon you and give you peace as you let the truths you've encountered in this study fill your mind and heart. And may you always love God above all else, seeking him with all your heart and mind and soul and strength. May you live devoted to loving God and loving his story.

Live in his love!

Notes

DAY 2: WORD

1 Britannica, The Editors of Encyclopaedia. "Logos." Encyclopædia Britannica, Encyclopædia Britannica, Inc., 21 May 2012, www.britannica.com/topic/logos.

DAY 5: RABBI

2 Deffinbaugh, Bob. "4. The First Disciples (John 1:35-51)." 4. The First Disciples (John 1:35-51) | Bible.org, 19 Aug. 2004, bible.org/seriespage/first-disciples-john-135-51.

DAY 12: SON

3 "Blasphemy." Merriam-Webster, Merriam-Webster, 2019, www.merriam-webster.com/dictionary/blasphemy. 6 September 2019.

Resources

ESV STUDY BIBLE

BLUELETTERBIBLE.COM

About the Author

Jazmin N. Frank is a Bible teacher and writer. Her heart beats to help women love God, love his story, and live beautifully devoted. She writes regularly at jazminnfrank.com where you can connect with her and find encouragement for all things Bible study, navigating your faith journey, and living freely as God's child.

STAY CONNECTED WITH JAZMIN

Facebook and Instagram

@jazminnfrank.com

Jazminnfrank.com

#beautifullydevotedlife

#beautifullydevotedcommunity

www.ingramcontent.com/pod-product-compliance
Lightning Source LLC
Chambersburg PA
CBHW051149290426
44108CB00019B/2664